DONCASTER
AND ITS RAILWAYS
THE SECOND SELECTION

DONCASTER
AND ITS RAILWAYS

THE SECOND SELECTION

PETER TUFFREY

TEMPUS

I would like to thank the following people for their help in compiling this book: Doug Brown, Miriam Burrell, Malcolm Crawley, George Firth, Jim Firth, Geoffrey Oates, Hugh Parkin, and Derek Porter.

Frontispiece: Women war workers involved in carriage duties during 1916. They are varnishing the golden teak body of this smoking carriage.

First published 2004

Tempus Publishing Limited
The Mill, Brimscombe Port,
Stroud, Gloucestershire, GL5 2QG
www.tempus-publishing.com

British Library Cataloguing in Publication Data.
A catalogue record for this book is available from the British Library.

ISBN 0 7524 2876 4

Typesetting and origination by Tempus Publishing Limited.
Printed in Great Britain by Midway Colour Print, Wiltshire.

Contents

Introduction 7

one The Plant 9

two In and Around Doncaster Station 59

three Views from the Lineside 89

four On Shed 113

five Railway Stations 121

six Industrial Locomotives 125

Great Northern Railway Merryweather fire engine on 19 December 1908. Members of the works' fire brigade are resplendent in their uniforms and brass helmets. The fire engine, while being horse-drawn, had a steam pump which could fire a jet of water for over 30m.

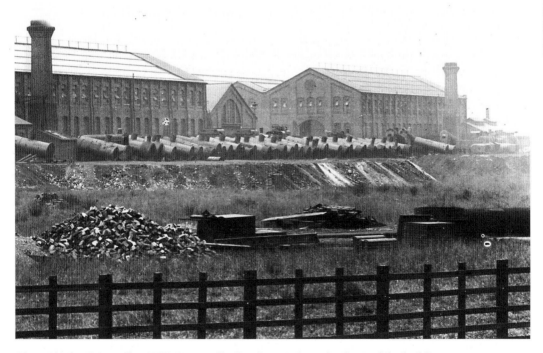

Alongside the Crimpsall, c.1905. Rows of boilers lie out along the front of the buildings.

Introduction

I am very pleased that Tempus Publishing has allowed me to compile another book on Doncaster and its railways. The last one was completed in the mid-1990s. It is particularly pertinent since the town's railway or plant works, noted for the construction of a number of world renowned locomotives, has recently celebrated its 150th birthday. The railways first came to Doncaster in the late nineteenth century.

The idea for the format of this book carries on from the one begun in the first volume, including pictures of people involved in the various jobs associated with the town's railways. I have also kept some of the chapter headings that appeared in the first book. One review that appeared about the latter was not very complimentary, yet quite a number of others understood perfectly my aim in compiling the book, with one actually stating quite boldly that 'it was spot on.' A number of reviews praised the inclusion of women carrying out a variety of railway duties. I am pleased to include a number of pictures featuring women, in what many may regard as a male dominated environment. But as a number of the photographs illustrate, this has not always been the case in Doncaster.

The dates of the photographs vary considerably, from around the turn of the nineteenth century to the latter years of the twentieth century. While some of the pictures are 'sharper' than others, I make no hesitation including those of a lesser quality, mainly because they show locations that were rarely photographed.

Quite a number of tasks that used to be performed around the plant are shown in the section featuring that area and I am particularly fond of the one showing foreman Charlie Parkin measuring a huge driving wheel. He would probably not have dreamed that in years to come he would be included in a book of this type, nor would he have predicted that his nephew, Hugh Parkin, would continue the Parkin family tradition of working at the plant, nor that Hugh would amass a great photographic archive of the area. Some of the older pictures and more modern ones in this book are from Hugh's collection and camera. Many of the 'official' pictures were taken by the works' photographer, Ben Burrell, who I was fortunate to meet and converse with on a number of occasions. He was a very friendly, likeable man and his daughter Miriam kindly allowed me to use some of his pictures.

Photographs taken in rare locations are mainly from the lenses of Geoff Warnes, Geoffrey Oates and George Firth. Geoff Warnes' pictures of the Garden Sidings signal gantry being demolished may be described as a unique piece of opportunism. But Geoff is noted for this. Other examples are the wagon works train approaching Hexthorpe Bridge and the Garratt at Barnby Dun. Geoffrey Oates is to be praised too for his splendid front end picture of the B17 locomotive, *Doncaster Rovers*, in Doncaster station. He is also responsible for the push-pull pictures at Denaby Halt and Harlington Halt.

Much of my own trainspotting was done near Hexthorpe Junction and from a vantage point (the bottom of a friend's garden) alongside Warmsworth cutting. So Geoff Warnes' pictures of steam locomotives in these locations bring back some happy memories for me. I therefore hope this book will evoke similar fond memories of Doncaster's railways from the distant and not too distant past.

Peter Tuffrey
January 2004

The exterior of a GNR mail van with staff, *c*.1900. Mail vans with sorting facilities first appeared on the GNR network in around 1849. It is believed that the horse was used for 'shunting' duties.

one

The Plant

Fitting staff outside D shop, c.1890.

Old tender shop cartridge case plant, 15 July 1915. Many munitions were made at Doncaster during the First World War.

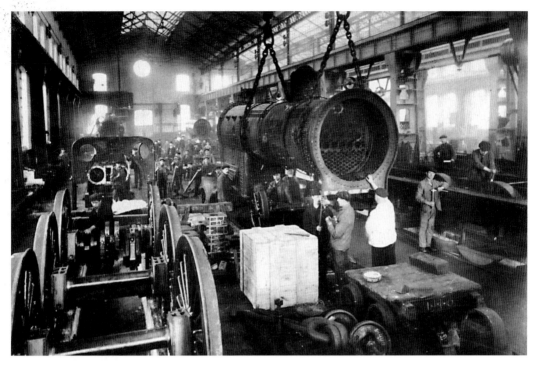

Ivatt Atlantics in the new erecting shop around 1905. The class originally consisted of ninety-three engines, built between 1902 and 1910. Of these, only seventeen survived into British Railways ownership in 1948. All were taken out of service by 1950, although the first, No.251, survives today.

In the official list of photographic pictures taken in Doncaster Works, this one is listed as No.32-23 and was taken on 19 February 1932. It is said to depict a scene in P shop showing 'skids for small tube reeling machine.' After the 1930 plant reorganisation, P shop (the tube repair shop) was located in the old Crimpsall tender shop. The area is known today as the dismantling shop.

Right: This photograph is numbered 32-44 and shows oxy-acetylene welding of boiler flue tubes in P shop, March 1932.

Below: 2-8-2 locomotive No.2393 is resplendent, having just left the paint shop with the Crimpsall in the background. This P1 Class locomotive took part in the Stockton & Darlington Railway centenary cavalcade soon after being built in 1925.

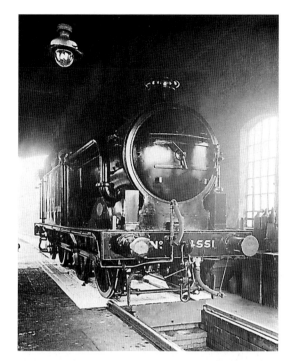

Left: Locomotive No.4551 in the old Weigh House, Doncaster Plant Works.

Below: 4-6-2 locomotive No.4495 *Great Snipe* at Doncaster Works. This A4 Pacific was used on the Silver Jubilee service. The A4 design was one of Sir Nigel Gresley's finest and the driving wheels were 6ft 8ins in diameter.

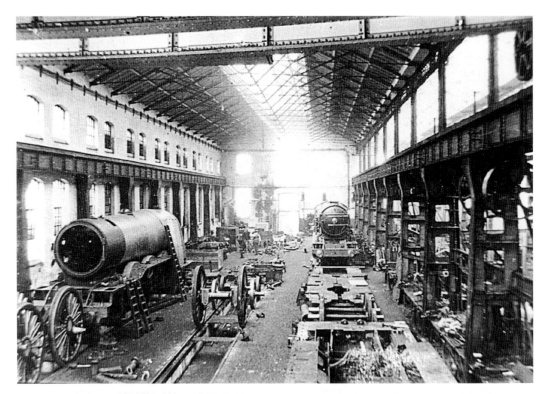

The new erecting shop during the 1930s.

Sparks fly! A foundation ring is welded.

A view taken of A4 locomotive No.4489 *Dominion of Canada*'s corridor tender, 6 April 1937. The building to the right is the works' paint shop. The corridor tenders were developed by Sir Nigel Gresley so that the A4s could travel non-stop all the way from London to Edinburgh. The crew could be swapped over part way through the journey by use of the corridor tender.

The diameter of a Pacific leading driving wheel is being measured here by the wheelshop foreman Charles Parkin (right) in July 1938. The flanged 'tyres' are still to be fitted. These were fitted by heating them up, placing them over the wheels and, when they cooled, they contracted on to the wheels.

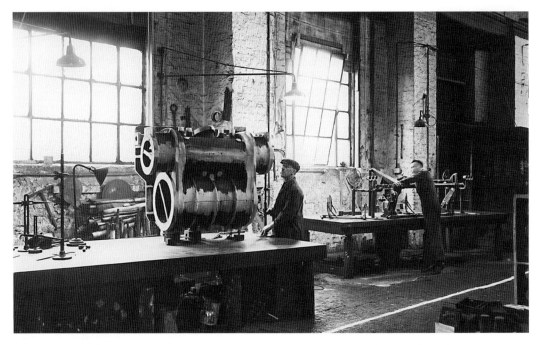

Work is taking place on the marking-off table in D6 shop during 1943. This cylinder is being finished off.

An A2 Pacific locomotive's conrod is being forged during the 1940s. The man on the left is senior blacksmith F.W. Robinson.

A4 locomotive No.4466 (originally named *Herring Gull*) is in wartime black on 4 January 1944, after being renamed *Sir Ralph Wedgwood*. The original A4 No.4469, named *Sir Ralph Wedgwood*, was damaged by a German bomb at York in 1942 and was withdrawn.

Women on war work, loading white-metal bars, 11 September 1944. White metal was used primarily for bearing surfaces in wheel boxes.

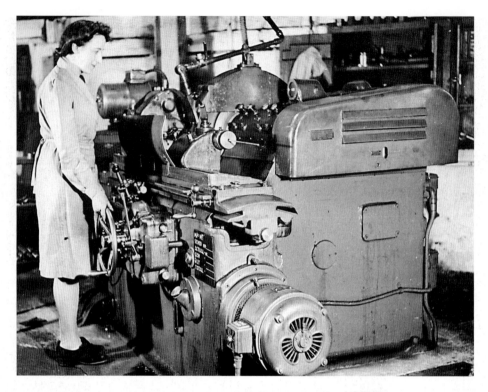

Two pictures of women war workers operating lathes in D shop during 1944.

Women war worker in a welding shop. Behind are bottles of oxygen or acetylene.

Plant coppersmiths pose for the camera on a day out to Skegness in 1948.

Class A2/2 Pacific locomotive 4-6-2 (former P2, 2-8-2 introduced in 1934), No.60505 *Thane of Fife* on 26 April 1950. The A2/2 locomotive weighed 101 tons 10cwt, and had 6ft 2ins driving wheels. This locomotive was photographed here in 1948. She carries her new British Railways number but still has her tender painted in LNER colours. The A2/2s were built as 2-8-2s for the express services from Edinburgh to Aberdeen, but were rebuilt by Thompson in 1943-44. By 1961 all of the class had been withdrawn from service.

Right: A1 locomotive 60133 *Pommern*, with the North Briton nameboard, 12 February 1951. Her shedcode was 37B, which denotes her home locomotive shed of Copley Hill, Leeds.

Below: The Locomotive Drawing Office take a lunch break at Harefield Hall during an outing on 30 May 1951.

The Doncaster Motive Power Depot's crane is employed on the works' scrap line during April 1952. A 20- or 30-ton boiler is being removed from the framework of a redundant locomotive.

Doncaster Locomotive, Carriage & Wagon Works centenary celebrations, 1853-1953. The event was held over the weekend starting 19 September 1953. The view is looking towards the Kirk Street entrance gates.

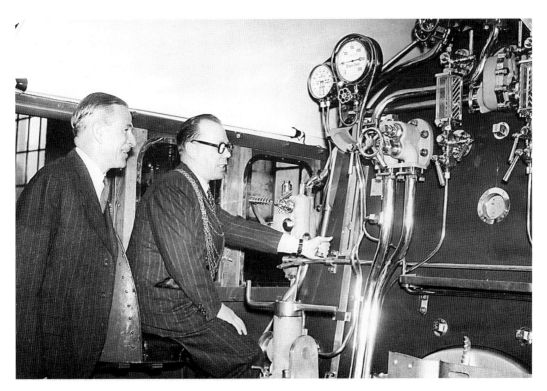

Mayor and Councillor A.E. Cammidge with R.A. Riddles Transport Executive, in a mock-up of a cab, located in the paint shop, during the 1953 plant centenery celebrations.

Doncaster Plant Works' centenary, 1953. A tiny works trolley has been converted into a 'Heath Robinson' affair for transport around the huge works.

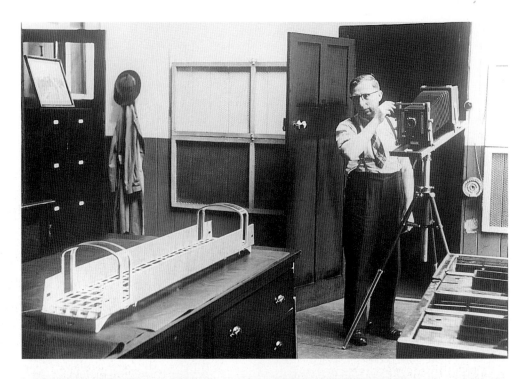

The plant's photographer, Ben Burrell, at work, 1959. The works' photographer was an important role, taking views of new designs and happenings in the works, as much for prosperity as to be used in British Railways publicity.

A1 Pacific *Boswell* preparing for trial-running at Weighhouse, 1959. On the right is another A1, No.60157.

2-6-2 V2 locomotive *Green Arrow* No.4771. Behind is a Riddles-designed 2-8-0 Wartime Austerity Class No.90024. After the war, the LNER purchased 200 of these locomotives. Together with another 533, which had been on loan to pre-nationalisation companies, these became Nos 90000-90774. Scrapping of the class began in 1959.

Above: The roof is being lowered onto a 25KV electric locomotive in E2 shop on 1 May 1961. By this time steam locomotive-building was dead in Britain's railway works and the advent of modernisation saw the rapid replacement of steam with new diesel and electric locomotives.

Right: A Derby Works-built DMU is being lowered on to its bogies in the DMU Repair shop on 4 October 1962. The body is being supported by two 20-ton travelling cranes, built by Craven Bothers of Manchester in 1901.

Opposite above: Locomotive office cleaning staff, *c.*1960.

Opposite below: Office cleaning staff, *c.*1960.

The joiners' shop, with carriage doors under construction, 1963.

Two AC Electric Prototype locomotives are seen with what was to become a Class 47 (centre) during 1963.

Mallard being overhauled in the Crimpsall's 4–Bay, *c.*1963. The insulation under her streamlined casing is getting a rare view of daylight. *Mallard* still survives in York's Railway Musuem.

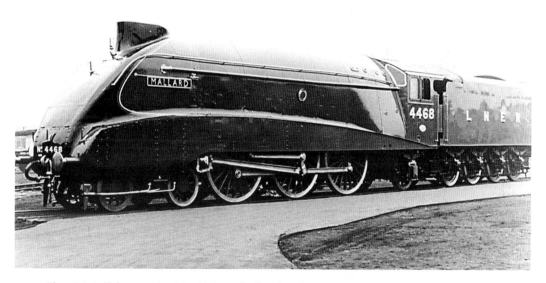

Class A4 4–62 locomotive No.4468 *Mallard* in the plant yard, *c.*1964. Her refit has finished and she has returned to her original LNER livery in readiness for preservation.

Class A4 4-6-2 locomotive No.60009 *Dwight D. Eisenhower* is at Doncaster Works during the 1960s.

The Spring shop prior to demolition in January 1965. As the needs of the railways changed, so did the works. The 1960s were a period of change as steam declined and the new modern railway lost the need for all sorts of traditional trades and buildings that had been part of the railway scene since the 1830s.

The old and the new. Class A3 4-6-2 locomotive No.60065 sits alongside the English Electric Deltic No.D9018 with the paint shop in the background. The Deltics were named after racehorses and famous regiments. A few have survived into preservation, and in a quirky turn of fate, some are now being used for main-line trains again through leasing companies.

Kirk Street canteen staff in December 1966.

Left: Miss *Rail News*, Miss Christine Weatherspoon, on a visit to the works on 9 March 1966.

Below: DMUs in the west shop on 66–359.

Opposite above: The wheel shop during November 1966.

Opposite below: The works manager's typing pool, 7 November 1967.

The Apprentice Training School intake, 1966/67.

34

Above: Ultrasonic wheel testing for hairline and unseen cracks.

Right: A wooden pattern for a wheel casting is being turned in M shop.

Construction work is being under-taken on a Class 56 locomotive. The first thirty locomotives were built by Electropute of Craiova. Thereafter the next eighty-five were erected at the plant, with the first emerging during April 1977.

The first Doncaster-built Class 56 No.56 031 is being lowered onto its bogies in the new erecting shop in the early part of 1977.

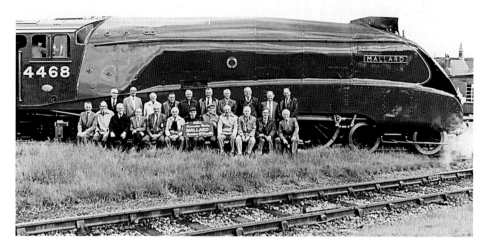

Mallard reunion, 10 June 1986. Retired staff are pictured in front of *Mallard*, which had been overhauled for main-line working and was seen regularly on the York-Scarborough run.

Open day stewards for 1994, Derek Porter, Eric Arnold, M. Crabtree, D. Wheeler, J.Walker and N. Daykin, are in front of *Sir Nigel Gresley*, the A4 Pacific named after its designer.

Class 47 locomotive No.47 522 *Doncaster Enterprise* alongside a Crimpsall paint team, which includes H. Dyer, M. Standage, O. Bean and Bob Ormshaw, during October 1987.

Malcolm Standage is fitting Doncaster's coat of arms to No.47522 *Doncaster Enterprise* in the late 1980s.

Above: Class 31 locomotive No.31 106 pictured after a heavy general repair in March 1988.

Opposite above: During 1990, new main entrance gates at the BRML Depot were made by the platers David Irvine and Mick Roberts and the welder Mick Brown. On the subject of the new gates, depot manager Ron Price said, 'First impressions are very important. Most successful companies owe nearly as much to a good image and profile as they do to a good quality product or service at the right price. The newly enhanced entrance certainly catches the eye of all approaching the depot for the first time. There can surely be no better shop window for displaying BRML Doncaster skills and abilities than an example of fine craftsmanship upon entry.'

Opposite below: A DMU is being repainted in the Crimpsall, *c.*1990. When introduced, the DMUs were popular with the travelling public. You could see the view from the front window past the driver, they were clean and, for the most part reliable. By the 1990s, the oldest were over thirty and the standards of service demanded by the travelling public were greater. However, there is no doubt that the DMU saved many a marginal branch line from closure, due to their cheapness of operation.

Brian Palmer is seen cleaning a Class 31 electrical cubicle in the paint booth wash area in 1A Bay, *c.*1990.

Manager H. Whitehouse and Shadow Transport Minister Claire Short with Hugh Parkin in the 1990s. Behind is an English, Welsh & Scottish Railways Class 56 diesel electric locomotive.

Above: In October 1991 a video crew
employed by Ruston Diesels hired a
section of BRML's 2-Bay at the
Crimpsall to film a newly overhauled
Class 56 locomotive power unit being
fitted into one of Trainload Coal's
locomotives. The intention of the
video was to show an example of the
Ruston diesel engine range and their
applications worldwide. Rustons
intended to use the promotional
video for both home and world
markets. Foreman Hugh Parkin
commented on the videoing, saying,
'It obviously sparked interest within
the shop and provided a talking point.
More importantly though, it gave the
film crew an appreciation of our jobs
and likewise it gave us an insight into
the way they work.'

Right: A BRML worker is under-
taking a drag box repair on
locomotive No.31 116 during
October 1991.

Locomotive No.31116 is fitted to bogies in the Crimpsall's 4-Bay during October 1991. Behind is a Class 37. It is interesting to compare images like this with those of the works in the days of steam. Cleanliness is the main difference and the disappearance of steam really improved the environment for the workers.

At a ceremony at BRML on 26 October 1991, the widely read *Rail* magazine had a locomotive named after it to mark the journal's tenth anniversary. The locomotive No.31 116, part of the Civil Engineer's Fleet, was painted in the new yellow and grey livery of the sector, following its overhaul at the depot. Judy Murray, Murray Brown and Jim Cornell (civil engineer) are seen officiating at the ceremony.

On 13 December 1991, a twenty-month project at BRML drew to a close, with a total of 336 Pacer Units for Regional Railways being fitted with direct acting brakes. The modification to the vehicles, which assisted in providing a more reliable service for Regional Railways, was welcomed by their director, Gordon Pettitt, seen here in the centre of the picture. Thanking BRML staff for their work, Gordon Pettitt said, 'Pacers originally had a poor reputation but since receiving direct acting brakes, they were vastly improved vehicles.' As the handing-over ceremony drew to a close, Depot Traction and Rolling Stock Engineer Dave Poulton presented Mr Pettitt with a model of the direct acting brake assembly.

During the early part of 1992, Doncaster BRML Depot had pleasure in welcoming Union Supremos Bill Jordan and Bob Elmson, who are seen here shaking hands, on a visit to promote the merger between the AEU and EEPTU. Bill Jordan congratulated the depot on its enthusiasm in meeting the changing requirements of customers.

In the early 1990s Class 305 EMUs were shipped to Doncaster BRML for the first time since they were built there in the 1960s. Regional Railways placed the contract for C3 overhauls for vehicles required for their service to Manchester Airport. The first four-car set, No.305515, was back in service by the end of 1993. One of the car sets is here with members of the BRML workforce.

Rail News reporter Steve Chapman is at BRML on 12 October 1993. He is photographing representatives from each trade, which under the leadership of Mick Georgeson, project manager, converted five former Class 121 'Bubblecar' units into Sandite/driver training vehicles for Network South East.

Depot manager Phil Crawshaw (right) hands a replica nameplate to councillor Colin Wedd during BRML Depot's open weekend, 'Railfair 800' – a rail safety weekend for charity held on 9–10 July 1994, as part of the town's 800 charter festivities. On Sunday, departmental shunter 08682 was named *Lionheart*. This name was particular fitting as it was Richard the Lionheart who had granted the town charter 800 years earlier. The ceremony was performed by councillor Colin Wedd, chairman of the 800 charter celebration.

The BRML Depot from the air during August 1994. In the distance, the plant's sports ground may be seen.

Left: Doncaster BRML came out top in the Inter-Rail First Aid final held in Llandudno during October 1994. The winning team, Chris McBride, Carl Chambers and reserve Alan Whitehouse, are here with the trophy. The team manager, David McArdle, is not pictured.

Below: Neil Daykin is fitting a pole piece to traction motor 10-1-90s.

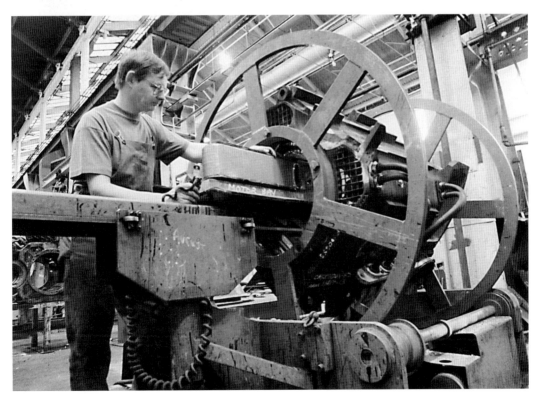

Opposite above: Chris Tyas is slinging Class 43 springs. An Inter City 125 is behind on the left.

Opposite below: In 1992, Patrick Stirling, a great-great-grandson of the famous locomotive designer, opened the Railway Housing Association's new Doncaster complex, called Stirling Court, not far from the plant. Patrick, a branch manager for the West Country Building Society, also took time to visit the BRML Depot and is seen here with depot manager Ron Price. Patrick was presented with a framed photograph of his great-great-grandfather and his supervisors, which was taken during the late nineteenth century.

Right: Master signwriter Colin Swindells at work, *c.*1994.

Below: Car 365 is passing the Rising Sun public house on its journey to ABB Doncaster on 5 November, possibly in 1994. Nowadays it is a common sight to see railway locomotives and carriages on the road network, as it is now often safer, cheaper and more convenient to move heavy loads like this by road rather than by rail.

Above: Inside BRML's Test House with locomotive No.43 095 undergoing running-in tests. The normally streamlined front is disrupted here as the emergency drawbar is out. With their streamlined fronts and lack of bumpers, the drawbars are a necessity for moving failed units or engines under repair.

Right: Sprinter Unit 158333, which was damaged in a collision with an HST at Newton Abbot in March 1994, arrived at Doncaster with a badly buckled front cab. The damage was so severe that it had to be cut away and rebuilt. Depot manager Phil Crawshaw praised all of the staff involved in completing the repair on time and under budget for the owners, Angel Leasing Co. The contract, worth in excess of £70,000, was awarded to Doncaster following an immediate site visit after the incident by technical resource members Geoff Bytheway, David Clulow and John Swain.

On time and on budget in July 1994. Metalworkers Tim Marsh, John Clothier and Mick Brown, who undertook the bulk of the work on the 158 Sprinter unit cab reconstruction, pose for the camera.

Roger Baker, project manager of the A4 Society, is pictured in the cab of *Sir Nigel Gresley* alongside 'new firemen' during BRML's open weekend in 1994.

On 29 September 1994, BRML Doncaster formally signed a contract with European Passenger Services for the design, overhaul and modification of twelve Class 37 locomotives. Here, the first of the Class 37s are being handed over by Phil Crawshaw, depot manager, to Mike Etwell, Director of Traction and Rolling Stock, in January 1995.

Hexthorpe Middle School closed as part of Doncaster Council's re-organisation plans in 1995. The plant charity committee donated £1,000 to their long-standing neighbours to boost the school finances and wish them well for the future. Dave Hall of the charity committee said, 'Doncaster Depot has grown up alongside the community and there are several strong links. It is a smashing school and it is the least we could do to give the children a great send off.' Here, Ian Parnell, Dave McArdle and Neil Taylor present the cheque to the youngsters of Hexthorpe First School on 3 March 1995. Obscured behind David McArdle is Dave Hall.

Right: During March 1995, three representatives from the Moscow Locomotive repairing works visited and toured Chart Leacon and Doncaster Maintenance Depots as part of an educational and cultural exchange visit. The Moscow Locomotive Repair Works, founded in 1901, was one of the oldest depots in the former USSR dealing with railway rolling stock. The works, which is a state enterprise within the system of the Ministry of Railways, specialises in the repair of suburban electric trains. The visit to the Doncaster Depot was hosted by depot manager Phil Crawshaw (second from right), on 20 March 1995.

Below: Several locomotives in and around the BRML Weigh House in the snow. They include a Class 37, a Class 56 and a Class 58.

Spotters' view from gates where several locomotives may be seen, including Nos 58 014 and 91 010. No.58 014 seems to be missing much of her engine.

'Houston we have a problem!' Chief foreman Lou Bailey investigates an exhaust leak on a newly installed Class 58 power unit at BRML.

Painter, M. Hodgkinson, fits decals to a Freight Co. Load Haul locomotive on 4 December 1995.

Regional Railways' No.158824 is at the Kirk Street gate after arriving from Cardiff with a seized drive on 4 June 1996.

The 08 shunter, *Lionheart*, draws a Class 56 locomotive from the Crimpsall's 2-Bay during a rather wintery day. About 7ins of snow cover the tracks.

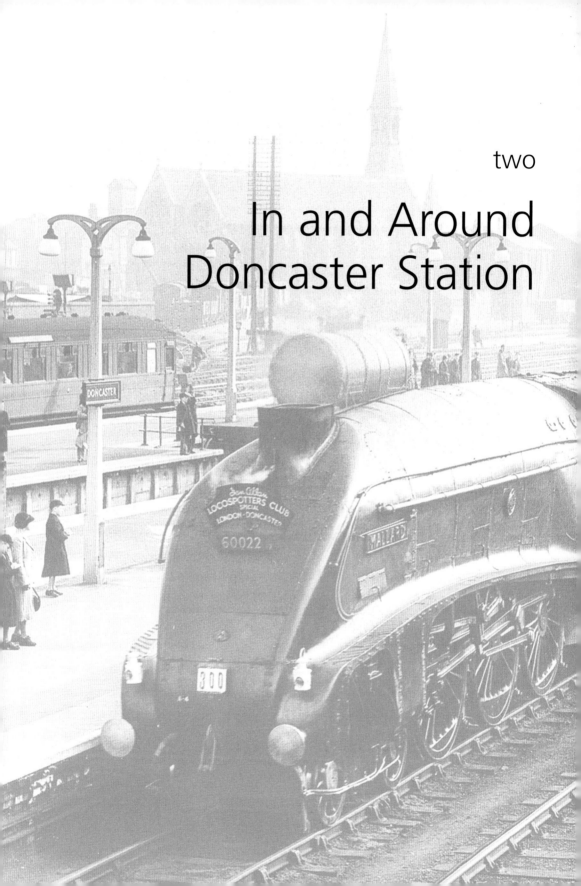

two

In and Around Doncaster Station

The preserved Midland Railway Compound locomotive No.1000 is leaving Doncaster on 30 August 1959. No.1000 was part of a class designed by Johnson and Deeley and built between 1901 and 1909. All were withdrawn between 1948 and 1953 but No.1000 was retained and preserved in her original condition, re-appearing in 1959 for use on enthusiasts' specials.

Peppercorn A2 No.525 is on trial and unnamed shortly after being built in December 1947, the last month of the LNER. The locomotive was subsequently renumbered 60525 and named *A.H. Peppercorn*, being withdrawn in March 1963. The driving wheels of these locomotives were 6ft 2ins in diameter and they had three cylinders.

Locomotive No.60153 heads a King's Cross-Edinburgh express on 2 August 1954. This was a slightly modified version of Gresley's A1 Class, and was called A1/1. All were built between 1948 and 1949.

After arriving in Doncaster with a train from Leeds, Class L1 locomotive No.67761 moves its complement of coaches to Garden Sidings during 1948. One hundred locomotives of this class were built between 1946-1950. They were two-cylinder 2-6-4T tank locomotives. The first four were built in 1946 and the rest between 1947 and, after nationalisation, in 1948. Scrapping of the class commenced in 1960.

Peppercorn Class A1 locomotive No.60146, without a nameplate, passes through Doncaster station with the *Queen of Scots* Express during 1949. The engine, completed in April 1949, was named *Peregrine* in December 1950.

No.61630 *Tottenham Hotspur*, a 4-6-0 engine of Class B17, is waiting for the 'all clear' signal on 7 April 1951. The colour light installation was a three aspect type with a route indicator which was used at Doncaster to control departures from Bay platforms. By 1960, all of this class had been withdrawn from service. Many of the class were named after football teams. The B17s were fitted with various different types of tender from NER, GNR and LNER origin.

Class J11 No.64403 is on Platform 'C' at St James' Bridge Station, in charge of a football special to Rotherham on 1 September 1951. The Class was introduced to the Great Central by Robinson in 1901 and the last was built in 1910. All of the class survived until 1954, but withdrawals began that year with at least fifty surviving until 1961 or later.

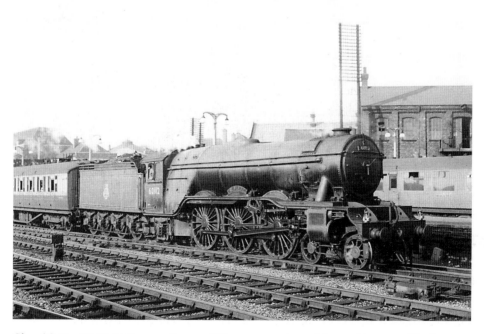

Class A3 No.60112 *St Simon* pulls out of Doncaster station while working on a King's Cross-Leeds express on 24 May 1952. The locomotive was completed in September 1923 as an A1 and rebuilt to Class A3 in August 1946. It was fitted with a double chimney in July 1958, trough deflectors in October 1962 and was withdrawn in December 1964.

Class 4-6-2 locomotive No.60122 *Curlew* approaches Doncaster station with a passenger train in the mid-1950s.

Locomotive No.62667 *Somme* is seen with the 5.16 p.m. Doncaster-Barnsley train on 12 September 1953. No.62667 was one of the eleven locomotives of Great Central Railway Class D11/1. They were built between 1920 and 1922 and the first to be scrapped was withdrawn from service in 1959.

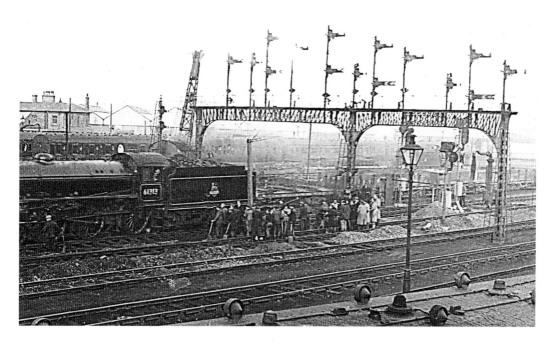

The signal gantry at Garden Sidings is in the process of being dismantled on 28 September 1952. In the first picture is locomotive No.61313, a Thompson B1 4-6-0. Construction of the class began in 1942 and the last was completed in 1950. These general purpose locomotives were as happy on passenger duties as they were with freight trains. They replaced a swathe of Atlantics from the GNR, NER and GCR, as well as various older 4-4-0s from the constituent LNER companies. The second view shows the gantry having had its signals removed and half dismantled. A steam crane prepares to remove the last of the gantry.

Class A3 4-6-2 locomotive No.60055 *Woolwinder* pauses at Doncaster station during the 1950s. Built in December 1924, the locomotive was never fitted with trough deflectors but had a double chimney from June 1958 and was withdrawn in September 1961.

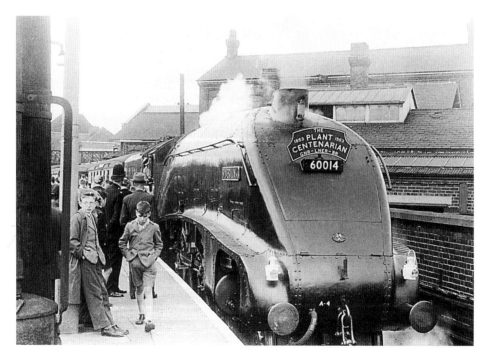

Class A4 4-6-2 locomotive No.60014 *Silver Link* is at platform 1 at Doncaster station, while working the plant's centenary during September 1953. Little interest is being paid to either the A4 or the photographer by the two young boys in the foreground.

Class V2 2-6-2 locomotive No.60858 approaches Doncaster station on 19 July 1954. The V2s, also known as Gresley's 'Green Arrow' Class, were introduced in 1936 for mixed traffic duties. They were, however, mainly used for express duties, being good steamers with a fair turn of speed.

Saddle tank No.68319 is taking water near Doncaster station with St James' church (known locally as the plant church) in the background during early 1950. Nos 68317 and 68319 were the last two survivors from 105 of a class of Stirling-designed 0-6-0ST engines, built between 1974 and 1891. They were originally constructed with domeless boilers. No. 68317 was scraped in 1948 and No. 68319 lasted until 1950, being sent to the breaker's yard soon after this photograph was taken.

Left: With her buffers proclaiming 'Up the Rovers', Class B17 4-6-0 No.61657 *Doncaster Rovers* is shown here at Doncaster station waiting to haul a special train to Middlesborough for the fourth round of the FA Cup away game on 6 February 1952.

Below: Class K1 2-6-0 No.62048 emerges from Hexthopre Bridge during the 1950s. The K1 Class was designed by Peppercorn and based on the K4 design by Gresley for the West Highland Railway. The class was constructed between 1949 and 1950.

Opposite above: Class A3 No.60046 *Diamond Jubilee* runs light engine towards Hexthorpe Bridge. The locomotive was completed in August 1924.

Opposite below: An unidentified Class A3 locomotive hauls a passenger train from platform 1 on to the main line during the late 1950s.

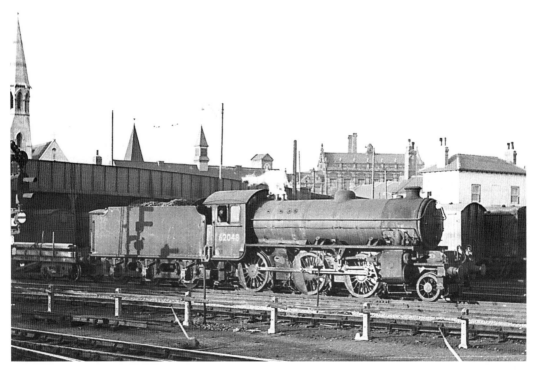

Class N2 No.69546 is in Doncaster station around the late 1950s. The N2 was a development by Sir Nigel Gresley of the HA Ivatt N1 Class with a larger boiler, superheater and piston valves. Fitted with condensing apparatus and shorter chimneys, some of the class were used on Metropolitan Railway widened lines, while a few locomotives of this class ended up in the Glasgow area. Withdrawal commenced in 1959 and, by 1961, over two thirds of the class had succumbed to the breaker's torch.

Class A4 4-6-2 locomotive No.60022 *Mallard* eases into Doncaster while working on the London-Doncaster Ian Allan Locospotters' Club Special in the 1950s. Eagle-eyed young trainspotters note down numbers as the train steams into the station.

Class A4 4-6-2 60007 Sir Nigel Gresley heads north while approaching St James Bridge, Doncaster, on 4 October 1959. Gresley, originally the Locomotive Superintendent and designer for the Great Northern Railway, was responsible for some of the most beautiful locomotives ever made in his A3 and A4 Pacifics, as well as *Mallard*, the fastest steam railway locomotive in the world and the most famous No.4472 *Flying Scotsman*.

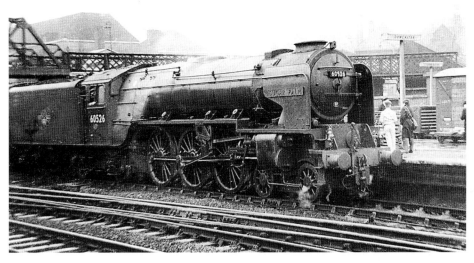

Peppercorn Class A2 locomotive No.60526 *Sugar Palm*, the second locomotive in the class, is in Doncaster station during the late 1950s. Built in January 1948, the locomotive was fitted with a double chimney in October 1949 and withdrawn in November 1962. The first two locomotives in this Peppercorn Class were the only ones to carry the LNER lettering on the tender sides. She is shown here with the early 1950s BR roundel logo.

Class A1 4-6-2 No.60139 *Sea Eagle*, a Darlington-built (December 1948) locomotive, approaches Doncaster with Denison House in the background. The locomotive was withdrawn during June 1964. To the left is the 'future', D5621, one of the new breed of diesel locomotives.

Class K2 No.61767 backs down through Doncaster station on its way to Doncaster Carr Locomotive shed on 8 August 1959. Some of this class (K2) ended up in Scotland and were named after Lochs. Built between 1912 and 1921, scrapping commenced in 1955 and five years later half of the class of seventy-four had gone.

The prototype Deltic eases its way out of Doncaster. The Deltic, so named after its unique engine design, was the future of rail transport. Built at Newton-le-Willows, it showed the potential of diesel to the bosses of British Railways. Designed as an express locomotive for the London-Edinburgh service, the Deltics were the flagship locomotives of BR in the same way as Gresley's A4s were the crack locomotives of the LNER. The prototype Deltic, in its fetching light blue livery, is to be seen today in York's Railway Museum.

Sir Nigel Gresley passing Doncaster station. This time the locomotive is working on a Stephenson Jubilee Special train.

Above: Midland Railway Compound locomotive No.1000 is leaving Doncaster on 30 August 1959, just after restoration.

Opposite above: An 0-6-0 saddle tank kicks out some exhaust while passing through Doncaster station in around 1959. This engine was one of seventy-five war department-type 0-6-0ST, purchased from the war department by the LNER in 1945. They were numbered 8006-8080 in LNER service and 68006-80 in their BR liveries.

Opposite below: This locomotive, pictured on 4 June 1961 near Hexthorpe Bridge, running light in reverse, was built as a Gresley A1 at Doncaster in April 1922, then rebuilt as a Thompson Class A1/1 in September 1945. Its first 1946 number was 500, and it took the number 60113 in October 1948. It was finally withdrawn in November 1962.

Locomotive No.63693 heads north through Doncaster station with a train of empties. Note the carriage cleaner in the distance on the right. No.63693 was designed by Robinson for the Great Central Railway and was one of a class of 2-8-0s built between 1911 and 1920. Many of the O4s were built for the Railway Operating Department for use during the First World War and then purchased by the LNER from 1924 to 1929. A large number of the engines went abroad again during the Second World War (including some of the same engines that saw service in France during the First World War) and these were not returned. 329 locomotives of this class came into British Railways ownership. They sold five back to the war department in 1952. Withdrawal of the rest began in 1959.

Class A1 locomotive No.60141 *Abbotsford* heads the Harrogate-King's Cross Pullman on 9 July 1961.

Class A2 locomotive 60536 Trimbush, ex-works, is passing Doncaster station on 29 April 1961.

Trainspotters are seen 'cabbing' Class V2 loco-motive No.60917 on Doncaster station's platform 5, on 9 August 1959.

The Doncaster–York–Darlington Flyer headed by locomotive No.1000, possibly in 1961.

Passing Doncaster south box is Class A1, 4-6-2 locomotive No.60117 with a down express. To the right of Doncaster South signal box is a diesel multiple unit.

Class A3 locomotive No.60061 *Pretty Polly* is heading north.

Class A3 locomotive No.60092 Fairway approaches St James Bridge with a passenger express. The locomotive was withdrawn during October 1964.

On 12 May 1963, the Warwickshire Railway Society ran a special which was headed by No.34094 *Mortehoe*. The locomotive is seen here near St James' Bridge. No.34094 was designed by another innovative locomotive engineer, O.V. Bullied, of the Southern Railway. Many of these locomotives were rebuilt and the streamlining removed (starting in 1957) but *Mortehoe* survived with her streamlined boiler casing. Normally running from London to Devon and the West Country, this locomotive is far from home. The first of the class was built in 1945 and the last in 1950.

Another Bullied design, locomotive No.35026, one of his larger merchant navy class Pacifics, with a Special, approaches Balby Bridge. Again, normally used on the Southern's express services from London, this merchant navy class locomotive is on foreign rails. By 1959 all of these locomotives had had their streamlining removed.

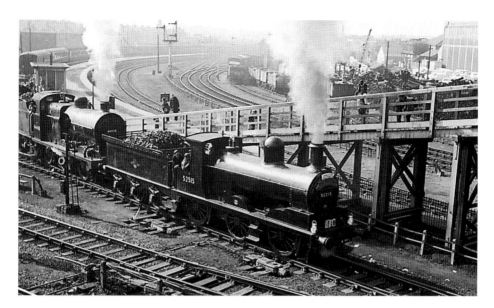

The ex-Lancashire & Yorkshire Railway locomotive No.52515 double heads the Midland Railway-designed No.44408 on a Special and is approaching St James' Bridge. Aspinall's L&YR design was built in large numbers from 1889 until 1917. Of the 246 survivors in 1948, about seventy of these 0–6–0s were still running by 1960. No.44408 was one of a class that extended to 772 examples built between 1924 and 1940, except for five built in 1922 for the Somerset & Dorset Joint Railway. Withdrawal of these 4–4–0s began in 1959.

Class A3 locomotive No.60051 *Blink Bonny* hauls a North Countryman Railtour train through Doncaster station at 7.48 a.m on 6 May 1964.

Above: Locomotive No.D6732 heads a Norwich City Football Club 'Canaries Special' in the late 1960s.

Opposite above: Class A1 engine No.60114 *W.P. Allen* is hauling freight on 24 October 1964. Note the ambulance on the wagon to the right.

Opposite below: Class A3 locomotive No.4472 *Flying Scotsman* with double tender is passing through Doncaster during 1965. At this time she had been restored to her 1924 LNER livery. *Flying Scotsman* appeared at the 1924 British Empire Exhibition at Wembley and also at the 1925 Stockton & Darlington Railway centenary celebrations.

Above: No.55 011 on a northbound express passing Doncaster station on 24 May 1978.

Opposite above: Deltic Locomotive No.55 008 heads an up express into Doncaster station on 3 August 1974. By 1981 the days of the Deltic were almost over as the class was withdrawn from service to be replaced by HSTs (commonly known as Inter City 125s).

Opposite below: No.45 002 hauls a special train of spun pipes at St James' Bridge, Doncaster, on 1 June 1977.

A3 No.4472 *Flying Scotsman*, arguably the most famous locomotive in the world, collects water at St James' sidings. *Flying Scotsman* was purchased from British Railways in the mid-1960s and was taken to America to be used for special trains in the USA. With her went the Pullman coaches that were used for Sir Winston Churchill's funeral train. Unfortunately, the whole business went bust and it was feared that the locomotive would be trapped in the USA forever. Eventually, she was brought back to the UK but the Pullman coaches were sold for preservation in North America. Within the past three years, two of the Pullman coaches have returned to the UK and have been extensively restored.

Doncaster station is seen from the town's northern bus station car park on 22 October 1993. In view is an 08 shunter, Class 56 and a Class 91 electric locomotive on an Inter City express.

Electric locomotive No.89 001 is on standby during July 1994.

Locomotive No.59 201 is passing platform 8 with a bulk freight train on 31 March 1995.

No.365535 is seen starting on a trial run to and from Peterbrough on 1 October 1996.

No.58 024 after a trial run to Newcastle on 14 November 1996. She is operated by English, Welsh & Scottish Railways, a freight operator.

three

Views from
the Lineside

An Ivatt 4-4-0 locomotive No.52 south of Doncaster on a short three–carriage passenger train.

Race traffic in the plant yard, *c.*1912. At this time, easy movement was by rail. There were few motorcars and tens of thousands went to the races by rail. The carriages will have been hauled by a mixture of types of engine, but these specials would have generated a small fortune in income for the Great Northern Railway. There are at least fourteen special trains in this shot!

A3 No.2570 Papyrus (later BR 60096) is pictured in 1935. The locomotive was built in March 1929 and withdrawn in September 1963. It received a double chimney in July 1958 and trough deflectors in Spetember 1961.

Class D49/1 4-4-0 locomotive No.245 *Lincolnshire* with a stopping train at Barnby Dun on 12 August 1946. All of this class were named after counties and were known as the Shire Class as a result. *Morayshire* still exists today. The Shires were slightly different from the similar Hunt Class, as they had Walschaerts valve gear as opposed to the Lentz valve gear of the Hunts.

Above: Class 7F No.49620 0-8-0 is leaving Harlington, while the push–pull service was halted on account of single line working, following the next signal box on 17 August 1951. 175 of these Fowler-designed locomotives were built between 1929 and 1932 for the LMS. Scrapping commenced in 1949 and, by 1961, only five of the class were still in service.

Opposite above left: Denaby sidings box with two tablets being exchanged.

Above right: WD locomotive No.90615 is on a section on the Dearne Valley Line. The driver is about to catch the single line tablet. For those unfamiliar with safe operation on single lines, a tablet was issued at the sidings box before a train entered a section of line. No other train could enter the section without the tablet thus rendering the line safe from collision. If more than one train was entering a section and travelling in the same direction, the tablet could be split so that they could all travel down. The next train in the opposite direction could not travel down the section until it had all the parts of the tablet.

In March 1903, it was announced that the contract for the construction of the third section of the Dearne Valley had been let to Gates & Hogg. The section extended from Thurnscoe to Denaby and Cadeby, a length of about six miles. The amount of the contract was over £100,000. The first two sections, extending from Brierley on the north and to Thurnscoe on the south, had already been constructed. The fourth section from Cadeby to Black Carr, south of Doncaster, was to be the next portion considered, and the total length of the railway, when completed, would be about twenty miles. The Dearne Valley Railway promised not only to play an important part in the development of the district, but to be an important connecting link between the West Riding and Lancashire railway systems on the one hand and the Eastern Counties and London on the other. The total cost of the line as given to the Parliamentary Committee in 1897 when the Dearne Valley Railway Act was legalised was just below £600,000 and it was not anticipated this figure would be exceeded. It was proposed that stations would be built at Grimethorpe, Houghton, Goldthorpe, Harlington, Cadeby, Warmsworth and Loversall, which would give an unrivalled access for produce both to the markets of the Eastern Counties and London and to the densely-populated centres of the West Riding and South Lancashire. The important collieries of Grimethorpe, Houghton, Hickleton, Denaby and Cadeby were upon or in direct connection with the line, and there would, therefore, be a very heavy mineral traffic to inland and export markets.

Left: A Dearne Valley Railway notice at Edlington Halt on 18 August 1951. These signs are now very collectable and this sign would be worth well over £100 today.

Below: Denaby sidings box, a Lancashire & Yorkshire Railway type, on the Dearne Valley Railway, 22 August 1952.

This passenger service began operating in 1912, linking the twenty or so miles between Wakefield (Kirkgate) and Edlington-for-Balby. At the beginning, it was worked by the Lancashire & Yorkshire Railway and its later successors (LMSR and LMR of BR). The service closed on 10 September 1951.

Locomotive No.41284 is hauling its single carriage train at Hickleton signal box. This locomotive was one of a design by Ivatt for branch line work. The first of the class of 2-6-2Ts was introduced in 1946 and construction finished in 1952.

Locomotive No.68778 is just south of Balby Bridge with the Vine Hotel public house at the top left. Built between 1892 and 1909, this design, by Stirling and Ivatt, eventually ran to 137 examples. No.68846 survived into preservation, but the remainder of the class had gone by 1961.

The Dearne Valley Railway line at Barnburgh on 24 May 1952. On the footplate of WD locomotive No.90631 are M. Chambers, Tony Peart and M. Fowler. (Photograph by Geoff Warnes)

Class B1 Locomotive No.61193 is at Hexthorpe, near Doncaster, heading a morning train bound for Liverpool on Saturday 4 December 1953. The first of this class to be scrapped was No.61057, which was destroyed in a collision at Chelmsford in 1950. (Photograph by Geoff Warnes)

Class J11 locomotive No.64386 at Hexthorpe on 31 October 1953. Designed for the Great Central Railway by Robinson, the first of this class was built in 1901 with the last in 1910. Some were superheated. All of the class survived until 1954, when withdrawal started. In 1961 about fifty J11s were still in service. (Photograph by Geoff Warnes)

Class B1 locomotive No.61314 near the North Bridge, Doncaster, is working a Hull train on Saturday 5 December 1954. (Photograph by Geoff Warnes)

Locomotive 4-4-2T No.67411 gathers speed at Hexthorpe with the morning train to Barnsley during March 1954. Designed for the Great Central Railway by Robinson, the C13 Class was constructed between 1903 and 1905. All survived until 1952, when the first were scrapped. The class was extinct by 1960 when No.67417 was withdrawn from service. (Photograph by Geoff Warnes)

Class A4 4-6-2 locomotive No.60017 is at Rossington with a Pullman train during the early 1950s. (Photograph by Geoff Warnes)

Class A4 4-6-2 locomotive No.60022 *Mallard* is just south of Balby Bridge with a 'reversed' headboard while working on an up express during the 1950s.

With a dusting of snow on the ground, a Robinson Class 04 locomotive fronting a train of empties approaches North Bridge during a cold winter's day in the 1950s. (Photograph by Geoff Warnes)

The 5.16 p.m. train from Doncaster to Barnsley is fronted by Class B1 locomotive 4-6-0 No.61166 at Hexthorpe Junction on 29 June 1953. The B1s had two cylinders and 6ft 2ins driving wheels. Designed as general purpose locomotives, they were as often seen hauling passenger trains as freight ones. (Photograph by Geoff Warnes)

Locomotive No.69904 fronts an oil train at Hexthorpe Junction on 10 May 1954. (Photograph by Geoff Warnes)

WD locomotive No.90436 at Barnburgh, *c*.1953. Used all over Britain during the Second World War, 733 of this class found themselves in British railway service after the war. (Photograph by Geoffrey Oates)

Class J52 0-6-ST No.68843 is taking empty coaching stock from the top yard at Hexthorpe Flatts to Doncaster station on 19 April 1954. (Photograph by Geoff Warnes)

An unknown Class V2 2-6-2 locomotive approaches the road bridge at Rossington during the 1950s. Used mainly for express main-line work, it was unusual to see this class on freight duties.

A Garratt locomotive is at Barnby Dun. This class of locomotives was built for the London, Midland & Scottish Railway between 1927 and 1930. Constructed by Beyer, Peacock & Co. of Manchester, they were designed for heavy freight duties and were probably one of the largest locomotive types ever to run in regular service in Britain. All of the class, except for Nos 47998-9, were fitted with revolving bunkers, as shown here. Scrapping commenced in 1955 and this class had disappeared from the railways of Britain by 1958.

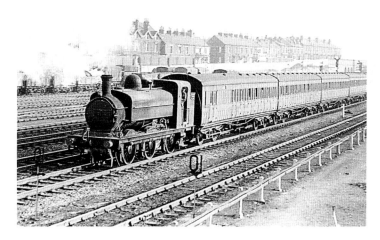

Class J52 engine No.68836 nears the end of its journey from the Doncaster Wagon Works, with a staff train on 18 September 1955.

A local man, Doug Brown, took this picture showing the 8 a.m. Sheffield Victoria-Doncaster train at Conisbrough railway station on 3 May 1955. The train is being hauled by a B1 Class locomotive. Kilners' Bridge is in the distance, once giving access to Cadeby Colliery but now providing a route to the Earth Centre. The station has seen many alterations since the time of the picture. On the right is the old freight avoiding line, which is now swept away. The line was also used for Sunday School excursions. There are no trees on the left and the trolley wires can be seen. Note also the upper quadrant semaphore signals, the shadow of the old lattice footbridge and the men with their 'pigeon' baskets.

Robinson locomotive Class No.63904 is passing Denaby Crossings, *c.*1960.

Class A3 4-6-2 locomotive No.60109 Hermit is near Bentley, north of Doncaster, heading the Yorkshire Pullman during the early 1960s. The locomotive was fitted with trough deflectors in January 1961.

Class K3 No.61891 trundles through Askern, north of Doncaster, c.1960. The K3s were a Gresley design for the Great Northern Railway. With 5ft 8ins driving wheels, these three-cylinder 2-6-0s were constructed between 1920 and 1937 and used for mixed traffic duties. The first of the class of almost 200 succumbed to the breaker's torch in 1950.

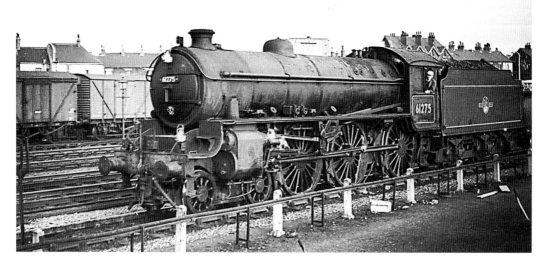

Class B1 locomotive No.61275 is at Garden Sidings during the early 1960s.

Class K1 locomotive No.62066 is at York Road running tender first. The K1 was a peppercorn development of Thompson's rebuilt No.61997 and was built between 1949 and 1950. (Photograph by George Firth)

Class B1 locomotive No.61044 pictured at Hexthorpe whilst working on a Hull-Liverpool train on 6 June 1961.

Directors' DMU Special Saloons, Nos E50416 and E56171, are in Doncaster Plant Works during 1966.

Locomotive No.34094 *Mortehoe* is on the Warwickshire Railway Society Special on 12 May 1963. This time the locomotive is at Hexthorpe Junction.

Class A4 engine No.4498 is on a special train north of Doncaster during the 1960s. Here she is painted in her LNER livery as she would have appeared in around 1939-1940.

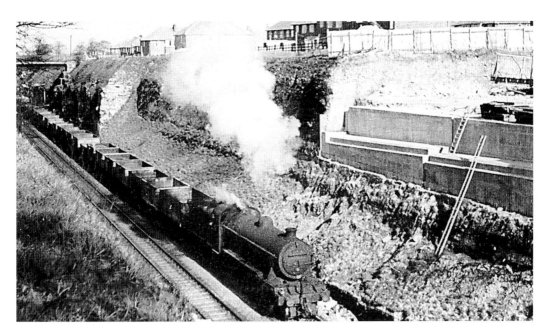

An 02/2 heads west along Warmsworth, cutting on the Sheffield to Doncaster line during the early 1960s. This was a Gresley-designed 2-8-0 with 4ft 8ins driving wheels and was constructed sometime between 1921 and 1934. This one is fitted with a GNR-style cab and tender. Later ones had LNER-style cabs and more modern tenders. Note the work taking place on the new A1 section of road extending between Blyth and Red House.

Warmsworth Cutting during the early 1960s with another 02 running light engine, this time awaiting signals before approaching Hexthorpe Junction. This one is fitted with LNER cab and tender.

A fine group of locomotives, including Deltic No.55 001 *St Paddy*, line up alongside Dennison House at Doncaster Plant Works.

Class 56 locomotive No.56 104 leaves Cadeby Colliery with the last MGR (Merry-Go-Round) bound for Eggborough Power Station on 12 June 1986. Albert Nelson, the driver, checks the load. The relief driver was Colin Rosser and D. Morgan was the guard.

Locomotive No.37 408 *Loch Rannoch* returns from a trial run on 22 February 1994. The locomotive is hauling the BRML trial train. It was photographed approaching Doncaster station by N. Daykin.

Brush locomotive No.31 466 runs light engine while the driver undergoes a route-learning course on 12 November 1996.

four

On Shed

Above: A formal group is alongside an Ivatt Atlantic locomotive at Doncaster Carr locomotive shed. The locomotive was probably new. This class of Atlantics was, for a time, the crack express locomotive type of the Great Northern Railway. The Atlantics numbered ninety-three and had 6ft 8ins driving wheels. Only seventeen reached BR service and only two of these received their new number before scrapping. No.68822 was the last of the class in ordinary service.

Right: Gresley Class A1 locomotive No.2543 *Melton* is in the Doncaster Carr coal hopper. The locomotive was completed at Doncaster in June 1924 and was rebuilt to Class A10 in May 1945, becoming Class A3 in September 1947. It was finally withdrawn during June 1963.

J52 locomotive No.68769 is with George Flowitt in the cab at the southern end of Doncaster Carr locomotive shed on 16 April 1952.

WD locomotive No.90696 is at Doncaster Carr locomotive shed on 25 April 1952. No.90732, the last in this class, was named *Vulcan*.

The view from the coal hopper during the 1950s. Note the 'turning triangle' in both pictures. In the top picture are nineteen locomotives including J6 0-6-0 No.64260, B1 No.61365, as well as a Class J52 0-6-0ST. The J6 Class were built between 1911 and 1922. Scrapping commenced in 1955 and, by the end of 1959, only forty remained of this class of over 100 locomotives.

Moving round, here is another view of No.64260, along with B1 No.61098 and Class S1/3 No.69904. The class consisted of only two locomotives and was a Gresley development of Robinson's S1/1 for the Great Central Railway. The 0-8-4T locomotive had 4ft 8ins driving wheels, three cylinders and was designed originally for shunting in Wath marshalling yard. There was a booster fitted to the rear bogie but it was later removed. This engine was scrapped sometime before 1957, having been built in 1932.

Views at the Doncaster Carr locomotive shed, looking over the boiler tops during the 1950s.

The view from the south of the Carr locomotive shed during the 1950s. Behind the shed is the coal hopper, which could fill a locomotive tender in one go. A wagon full of coal was lifted to the top of the hopper, emptied by turning it upside down and the coal was fed into the tender.

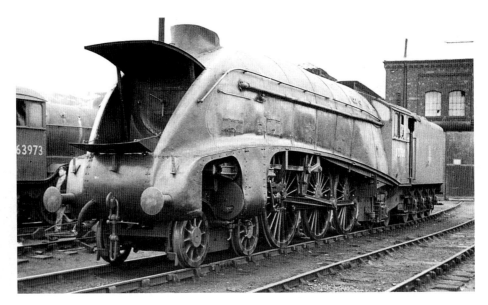

Locomotive No.60700 is at the Doncaster Carr locomotive shed during the 1950s. Her streamlined casing is open and her smokebox door is clearly visible. No.60700 was a rebuilt version of No.10000, Gresley's 4-6-4, 4-cylinder compound with water tube boiler, express passenger locomotive. She was rebuilt, as shown here, with a more traditional A4-type streamlining in 1937 and converted to 3 cylinders. This locomotive, once the most powerful passenger locomotive in Britain and the only 4-6-4 built for Britain's railways, was scrapped in 1959. Behind is a Class O2 2-8-0 No.63973.

A3 locomotive No.60099 *Call Boy* shortly before receiving trough deflectors in July 1961. Just over two years later the engine was withdrawn from service and scrapped.

Peppercorn Class A1 Pacific No.60157 *Great Eastern*, which was built at Doncaster in November 1949, is on the Doncaster Carr locomotive shed turntable, *c*.1960.

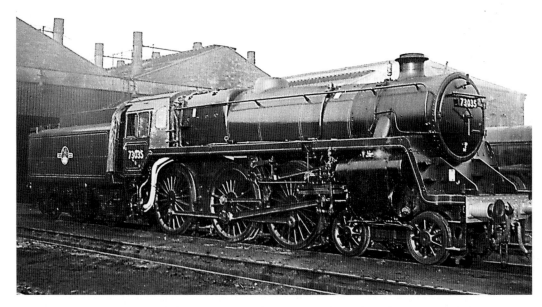

Locomotive No.73035 is on shed at Doncaster. This was one of British Railways' standard designs. The Standard Class 5 mixed locomotives were 4-6-0s, based largely on the similar LMS design introduced by Sir William Stanier in 1934. The BR version first appeared in 1951 and construction ceased in 1957. 172 were built, of which Nos 73125-73154 had Caprotti valve gear. The class had 6ft 2ins driving wheels and two outside cylinders.

A Great Central locomotive is with staff at Mexborough Shed.

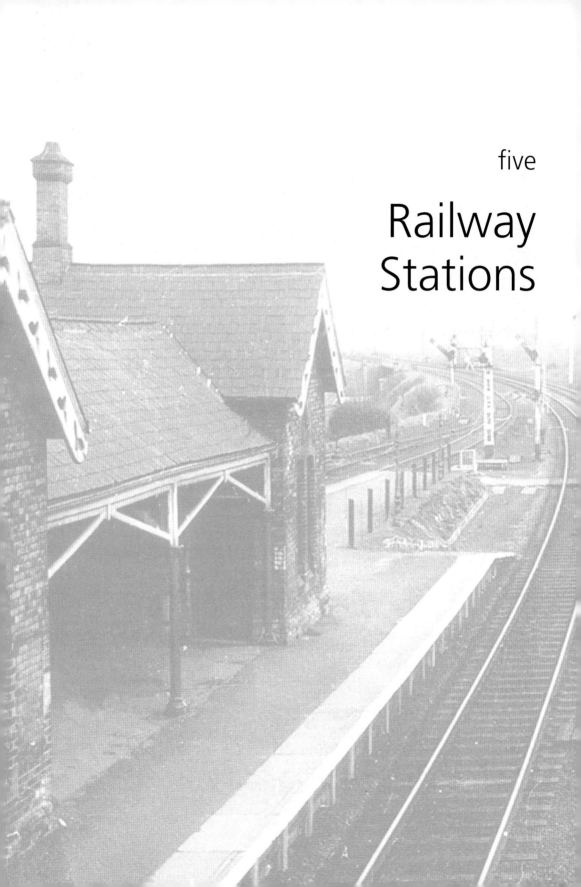

five

Railway
Stations

During March 1883, it was stated in the *South Yorkshire Times* that the new railway station, which was in the process of erection at Conisbrough, would, it was estimated, be completed on around 1 August. Additionally, there was to be a commodious house erected for the station master and general offices. The scheme also included a bridge for passengers, which would extend from the up platform to the turnpike road, so that passengers would no longer have to cross the line. At first it was contemplated to make a subway, but the engineers met and decided that it was more advantageous to have a bridge. In connection with the new station there were many improvements, not the least important of which was to be the construction of new sidings. The plans of the work were drawn up ten years earlier, but were not followed through at the time as a consequence of the negotiations for the making of a new line from Warmsworth to Shireoaks. If the latter scheme had been carried out the station would have been erected nearer the village than the present one, and a junction effected with the new line. The Manchester, Sheffield & Lincolnshire Railway Co. proceeded with the old plan, and spared no expense on the station. The existing station was to be pulled down, and its site occupied by sidings. The work was carried out by Mr Wortley of Doncaster.

Harlington halt station on 26 July 1951. It was a typical example of the station building found on the Dearne Valley Railway. It is certainly one way to re-use a redundant wooden framed and bodied carriage.

In recent years the railway station underwent some demolition and modification.

Locomotive spotters at Rossington station watch as Class K3 locomotive No.61964 trundles past with a mixed goods train

Demolition is taking place at Rossington station.

Finningley Station on the Doncaster to Lincoln line.

six

Industrial
Locomotives

Above: Hatfield Colliery locomotive No.6 ex-Appleby Frodingham 0-6-0ST on 28 December 1953. This 0-6-0 Saddle tank came into Coal Board service from the steel works at Appleby-Frodingham near Scunthorpe.

Opposite above: Three standard gauge diesel locomotives at Cadeby Colliery. The national Coal Board had a large fleet of locomotives for shunting wagons within their collieries. In some collieries, steam lasted until the mid-1970s, before being replaced by diesel locomotives.

Opposite below: Hatfield Colliery locomotive No.5 ex-GSWR (1917) on 28 December 1953. The locomotive was originally built for the Glasgow & South Western Railway before being purchased for use in the colliery. Hatfield No.5 was an 0-6-0 Side Tank with twin outside cylinders.

Other local titles published by Tempus

South Yorkshire Collieries

JOHN GOODCHILD

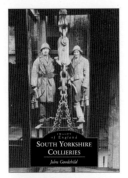

Coal has been mined in parts of South Yorkshire for centuries but it is the last hundred and fifty years that have seen the greatest expansion of the industry. Improvements in technology and techniques led to the growth of the coalfield, especially around Doncaster, as mines reached greater depths. Parallel to this development was the advent of photography, which has left a unique visual record of the coalfield.

0 7524 2148 4

Doncaster and its Railways

PETER TUFFREY

This fascinating collection of over 200 photographs illustrates Doncaster's role in the history of the railways, from the early images of locomotive construction in the 1890s at the Doncaster Plant, through the glorious days of steam to diesels and electrics.

0 7524 0635 3

The South Yorkshire Coalfield History and Development

ALAN HILL

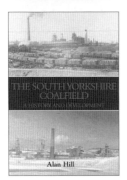

What made the South Yorkshire Coalfield important was its size. The area covered was huge, running from Barnsley to Sheffield and Doncaster and beyond. It also held some of the richest seams in England, the most important being the Barnsley, Parkgate and Silkstone seams. Inside *The South Yorkshire Coalfield* is the history of this once proud industrial area and of the mines that were worked within its geological boundaries.

0 7524 1747 9

The Sheffield & South Yorkshire Navigation

MIKE TAYLOR

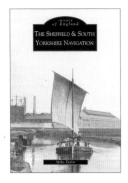

From the improvements around Sheffield at the end of the nineteenth century, through neglect during the First World War, public ownership and the expensive modernisation scheme of the 1980s, as well as the triumphs and failures of private enterprise, *The Sheffield & South Yorkshire Navigation* documents the history and development of the waterway.

0 7524 2128 X

If you are interested in purchasing other books published by Tempus, or in case you have difficulty finding any Tempus books in your local bookshop, you can also place orders directly through our website

www.tempus-publishing.com

or from   **BOOKPOST**, Freepost, PO Box 29, Douglas, Isle of Man, IM99 1BQ
tel 01624 836000   email bookshop@enterprise.net